FROM STROKE TO RECOVERY
MY WALK WITH GOD

A GUIDE TO RECOVERY

KIM BLACKWELL

Copyright © 2019 by Kim Blackwell.

ISBN   Softcover   978-1-950580-21-7

All rights reserved. No part of this book may be reproduced or transmitted in any form or by any means, electronic or mechanical, including photocopying, recording, or by any information storage and retrieval system without express written permission from the author, except in the case of brief quotations embodied in critical reviews and certain other non-commercial uses permitted by copyright law.

New King James Version (NKJV)

Scripture taken from the New King James Version®. Copyright © 1982 by Thomas Nelson Inc. Used with permission. All rights reserved.

Printed in the United States of America.

To order additional copies of this book, contact:
Bookwhip
1-855-339-3589
https://www.bookwhip.com

I dedicate this book to my wonderful family—my mother, Mildred; my siblings, Leslie, Vernice, and Venord Mark; and my nieces and nephews, Dawn, Christopher, Dr. Jonathan Wooden, Chandler, and Trey—for their love and support.

CONTENTS

Foreword vii
About the Author xi
Acknowledgments xiii
Introduction xv
Preface xvii

Chapter 1. Important Events in Her Life 1
Chapter 2. The Hospital 9
Chapter 3. Therapy 15
Chapter 4. He's Always There 23
Chapter 5. The Access Experience 27

Conclusion 31
Appendix 1: Scriptures She Confessed Daily 33
Appendix 2: Songs that Comforted Her 35
Appendix 3: Books that Inspired Her 37
Appendix 4: Resources/Information 39
Appendix 5: Photos 45
Endurance 53
Chuks Echiemeze Okoye Biography 57

FOREWORD

LIKE KIM MONICA, I am a woman who has walked with God through trial to triumph! With the unforeseen death of my mother in May 2014, separation from my husband in September 2014, and his sudden death in November 2016, I have weathered insurmountable emotional and financial odds. But God! He has led us every step of the way, and he promises to *never* leave us or forsake us! That is a promise that we not only hold dear but also have come to embrace as absolute *truth* ! God's love for us has kept us on our feet and propels us forward to victory!

Kim made a *decision* to recover her life to wholeness. What are significantly the same about a physical fight to recover and a financial fight to recover are the following:

1. One must remain emotionally stable in order to persevere. Know that the precious Holy Spirit is your comfort and your guide!

2. You must keep going no matter what!

3. You must rise above fatigue, frustration, disappointment, and regret in order to obtain the results you are seeking! I can't promise you an easy road ahead, but once you've ironed out the details, like Kim, you can live out your life in wholeness.

In this book, Kim shares how she challenged the system for her rights to receive various aid and assistance, all the while fighting for justice, not only for herself, but also for *you* who have invested in this publication.

With every encounter, she was not only determined to win and obtain the assistance she needed, but she committed to document her journey and pass on her experience to others so that you would not have to endure the pain and suffering she bore while being patient with the process. She obtained every tool she needed to fully recover—both physically and financially.

I too challenged the system and fought a major health plan company for the wrongful death of my mother. That process was lengthy, arduous, and designed for my defeat. But God! The grace of God *carried* me to victory through difficult tasks and dark days. His grace is sufficient for us because his strength is made perfect in our weakness; in other words, when we can't see around the next bend, we can trust him and remain at peace, knowing that all we need to do is *have faith in God, keep moving forward toward the goal, and never give up!* Although Kim faced days of physical struggle, God's grace kept her mind strong, so she had the ability to think clearly and handle much of the research and administrative tasks on her own, *and so can you!*

Use this book as a guide to maneuver through every task required to realize victory and to *fully recover all* ! Regain your whole life. Don't leave any of God's goodness in the devil's hands. What is intended for you is there for you—just reach for it and believe God to see you through. Allow Kim to share with you her story, and glean from her research. She will save you time and much heartache!

From Stroke to Recovery My Walk with God, A Guide to Recovery will place you on the path of recovering everything you lost after the devastation of *temporarily* functioning outside of a place you never thought you would be. I witnessed Kim's recovery over time. I watched her storm the doors of agencies, in the form of phone calls and letters, again and again until she received the answers that she sought. Allow her efforts to help you take back *everything* that belongs to you so that you may live your best life ever! In this book, Kim gives you the tools to go forward, and her story will help you to see the brighter side of life as you regain your composure and stand strong!

The Lord bless you and keep you!
Rhonda Alford

ABOUT THE AUTHOR

KIM BLACK WELL'S ENTREPRENIAL spirit and desire to help others was inspired by her grandparents, who owned two dry cleaners and a variety store in Philadelphia Pennsylvania. Her memorable encounter with a special needs child, while working at the variety store, led her down a life path of service. As a sales representative, Kim aided families in securing their financial futures by selling life insurance and investing their money in IRAs. Kim later facilitated the preparation of effective advertising campaigns for real estate companies and agents at the Los Angeles Times finally, as the founder and owner of unique designs she marketed and distributed artwork for African and African-American artists along the West Coast. She coordinated art and trade shows for her artists Work and created unique designs.com and the unique designs cable television show to display their impeccable creations.

Now as the author of *From Stroke to Recovery, My Walk with God, A Guide to Recovery* Kim Blackwell shares her many challenges and victories of the massive stroke she suffered in 2008 which changed her life forever. By telling the story of her miraculous walk toward revival, and her faith and trusting God knowing that he would see her through, Kim aims to use her journeys many challenges to help others with the process of recovering their lives.

ACKNOWLEDGMENTS

SHE WANTS TO thank all her therapists at Providence Holy Cross Medical Center in California and those at MossRehab at Einstein in Elkins Park, Pennsylvania. She wants to thank Apostle Price, Pastor Fred Price from Crenshaw Christian Center, for teaching her the Word of God, and she wants to thank Pastor Cheryl Davis for following her heart and starting a Bible study that is like no other.

Finally, she wants to thank her friends and neighbors: Tammy, Karyn, Brenda, Rhonda, Keeley, Joscelyn, Randy, Anna, Gastone, Robert and Doug.

INTRODUCTION

THE AUTHOR WAS born Kim Monica Cowan on August 26, 1957, at Mercy Fitzgerald Hospital in Lansdowne, Pennsylvania, to Venord and Mildred Cowan. She is one of four children; her siblings' names are Leslie, Vernice, and Venord Mark. They are a very close family, and her parents instilled in them the importance of family and gave them a firm spiritual foundation. Her father's father and grandfather were preachers. They attended church every Sunday, and her father was a very active member in the church. The Bible says in Proverbs 22:6 (NKJV), "Train up a child in the way he should go and when he is old he will not depart from it." As a child, she believed in God, Jesus, and the Holy Spirit. She remembers learning the most about the Bible during confirmation at thirteen, but she would have never imagined that she would know God the way she does now.

PREFACE

THE WORD RECOVERY represents not just getting back her physical body but obtaining the things she would need to get her life back, the author tells of her miraculous recovery and her faith and trust in God, knowing he would bring her through the many challenges she would face to obtain what she had worked many years for. With her determination and perseverance, she endured until she obtained everything she needed to make herself whole again: income, health insurance, and transportation. This book will provide insight into the process of recovery to help others avoid the unnecessary pitfalls that she went through. Her goal is to eliminate the question for others of . . .

What do I do next?

CHAPTER 1

Important Events in Her Life

KIM ATTENDED DUQUESNE University in Pittsburgh, Pennsylvania, in 1975.

She chose Pittsburgh because her sister Vernice was attending Carlow College there. But God had California in his plan for her. She had gotten accepted to the University of California in Los Angeles, but she could not go because it was too far away. But God had his own plan. In her freshman year at Duquesne University, she met Nelson Blackwell, who was from Philadelphia. He was a good-looking, smart, funny, kind, adventurous, and good person. Kim graduated in 1979. She planned to go to graduate school at Pace University in Upstate New York. Another cold state? No way.

Nelson had a sister who lived in California, so he had planned to go there. Kim was young and could go to graduate school anywhere. So she decided to go to California with him in October 1979. That was a big change, not having family there, but she went anyway. Over the years, she would have a wonderful extended family, which included many friends. There were a couple of statements that she heard about Southern California that were not true: one is that it never rains in Southern California, so in February, when it did, she was quite surprised. First impressions are everything. When she would say hello to people while walking down the street and they did not say hello back, she would say to herself, "Who are these people?"

She got accepted to Mount Saint Mary's College in their graduate program.

Getting Married in 1980

She went back to Philadelphia to get married in November 1980. Now, her name is Kim Monica Blackwell.

The Los Angeles Times 1984

Every Sunday, she would read the *Los Angeles Times* newspaper and look at the advertising ads and thought, *How do the ads get in the paper? How does the whole process work?* One day, she would love to work at the *Los Angeles Times*. She decided that that would be her next job. So she went to the local newspaper and applied for a job as a sales representative and got a job at Coast Media Newspapers that published ten local newspapers. The Olympics were held in Los Angeles, and she sold an eight-page tabloid section for the newspaper. Once the section printed, she created a portfolio and went to apply for a job at the *Los Angeles Times*. She got her dream job as an advertising sales representative with the *Los Angeles Times*.

In 1986, they bought a townhome in the San Fernando Valley.

In 1987, her parents came to visit, and she celebrated her father's sixty-third birthday. The next night, her father would have a heart attack and died at the hospital. That was one of the worst times in her life. Nelson took care of everything to get her back to Philadelphia.

She was very active and went to the gym, and she played basketball with a women's league.

In 1990, she had a major knee injury while playing basketball. Thank God for Nelson being in her life at that time; he found a doctor who specialized in sports injuries. The first thing the doctor asked her was, "Do you want to play basketball again?" And she said yes. For the next nine months, she came home from physical therapy in tears. It was so painful, but she was determined to get better. Nelson would come home from work and prepare meals for the week, and on weekends, he called it driving Miss Kimmie. After all the hard work and tears, on Thanksgiving Day in 1991, she got on the basketball court again. She decided not to go back to play with the women's league because she had achieved her goal. In 1992, she found her church home Crenshaw Christian Center.

In 1994, she started Unique Designs. She loved art, music, and movies. She attended the Pan African Film and Arts Festival, and there were so many talented African and African American artists there that she had never seen before. She spent the day talking to the artists and buying some of their beautiful creations. She thought to herself, *Why had she never seen these guys before?* She wanted to help them get exposure on the West Coast. With her advertising, sales, and marketing background, she started a home-based business called Unique Designs where she distributed artwork of African and African American artists along the West Coast. She exclusively represented artists Chuks Okoye, Ron Witherspoon, and George Nock; and she carried the artwork for the following artists: Kelvin Curry, Sharon Geri-Boyd, Designs by Sandy, Cidne Wallace, Buchi Upjohn, William Tolliver, Carl Anderson, Kathleen Wilson, Reginald Webster, and Shelton Gillis. The avenues of distribution were a website called UniqueDesigns.com, art and trade shows, and finally, the Unique Design cable TV show. That same year, she experienced her first earthquake. She was home alone that day. Nelson had gone with his friends on their annual trip to Lake Tahoe.

A couple of months before, she had been putting her earthquake kits together for the home and her car, so she was prepared. Nelson flew back right away. She was able to get out of the house and drive to her sister-in-law's in Los Angeles. She did not panic but went into action, stayed calm, and did what she needed to do.

Divorce in 1999.

In 2000, she went to Rome, Italy, with her mother. In 2001, she attended UCLA and received a professional designation in marketing.

She admits that a physical injury of any kind does not compare to the pain of a broken heart. Only God can heal that. She was glad that her relationship with God was just beginning to develop. Her comfort came from being in the Word of God, spending time listening to tapes and CDs on subjects like love, forgiveness, healing, and most importantly, how much God loved her. She attended seminars, watched pastors on TV, and sucked up God's Word daily. She believed God's Word in Deuteronomy 31:6 (NKJV), which says, "He will never leave you nor forsake you." Psalm 119:105 (NKJV) says, "Your word is a lamp to my feet and a light to my path." Acts 17:28 (NKJV) states, "In him I live and move and have my being." She went to church pretty consistently but not every Sunday. She was learning a lot about the Lord and how to apply the Word in her life. She did not date anyone for four years. She had a few male friends that she went out with, but she was not in a relationship. She prayed and waited for the right man. She was very busy with work and her business, and she traveled to other cities sometimes to work with her artists at various art shows. In 2005, she told God that she wanted him to work in every area of her life. She thought to herself, *What are you asking God to do?* Malachi 3:10 (NKJV) says regarding tithing, "'Bring all the tithes into the store house so that there may be food in my house and try me now in this,' says the Lord of host, 'if I will not open for you the Windows of heaven and pour out for you such blessing that there will not be room enough to receive it.'" Her revelation came from two words: *try me.* "Do what my word says by faith, and you will see that it works." God has already done everything he's going to do. She committed to going to church every Sunday and Bible study once a week, attended all events at the church, and went to other churches on special occasions. As a sales representative at the *Los Angeles Times*, she was very busy and always in need of divine intervention. She wanted to increase her sales at the *Los Angeles Times* and do something different with her business. She needed a new avenue to market the artwork. By this time in her life, she was going to God about everything, so she prayed about it. Regarding her job, she asked God what to do. He said, "Go back to the basics," which meant doing more cold-calling, attending more real estate meetings, and preparing more sample ads to show real estate agents. She looked at her business and asked God what she could do differently. Early one morning, she woke up and wrote pages on what the Unique Designs cable TV show would be about. It would be an interviewing format with artists and people who had products and services that were unique. The show would be educational and informative.

At the *Los Angeles Times* that year, she won the *Los Angeles Times* Classified San Fernando Valley Real Estate Division Award for top revenue producer of the year. That same year, she went to Brazil with her girlfriend Karyn and her mother to celebrate her fiftieth birthday. These are examples of her asking God to help her, and he did. Isaiah 55:11 (NKJV) says, "So shall my word be that goes forth from my mouth it shall not return to me void but will accomplish what I please and it shall prosper in the thing for which I sent it."

Then God started to put the people around her that would make it happen. She had been volunteering at an organization called Helpers for the Homeless and Hungry. The organizer was Mrs. Humphrey. She did not know that she had been a member of her church. She had a cable TV show and invited her on the show to feature the artwork. Mrs. Humphrey was friends with a producer named Felix Washington, who owned a recording studio. She told him about her idea for the cable TV show, and he thought it was a great idea and offered to produce it for her.

Fast-forward to 2007.

She met Tammy Yelling at a homeowners' association meeting. She had been living in the complex for seven years, and she had never met Tammy. She would become one of her best friends and introduced her to a wonderful Bible study group. The only thing that she was planning that year was her fiftieth birthday celebration in August.

In March, the *Los Angeles Times* offered a buyout. It was based on the number of years she had been with the company. This was the best buyout the company had ever offered. She had been with the company for twenty-two years. If she took it, she would stay on the payroll for ten months with benefits. She considered applying for it so that she could work on the cable TV show full-time. It was unlikely that she would get it because she worked in a small real estate advertising department, and she was a top producer. She prayed and asked God if she should apply. She got a word from God, "Yes, apply for it." She applied, and she got it. Her boss said he did not want to sign it, but he did not want to be the one to keep her from pursuing her dreams. The director of real estate advertising said she did not want to sign it because she thought she would be making a mistake, but she signed it and wished her the best.

In April, she was diagnosed with high blood pressure. It was strange because she ate chicken, turkey, and fish when she cooked, and she worked out three times a week. But she was an outside sales representative, so she could not always eat healthy in the field. In June, she left the *Los Angeles Times*. In August, she celebrated her fiftieth birthday with family and friends in Barbados and had a great time. In November, she was rushing to go to a birthday party and fell down the stairs and hit her head on the wall so hard she could hear it ringing. She got up and looked in the mirror, and there was a large contusion on her head. She began to pray in the spirit and called 911. When they got there and saw the size of the contusion on her head, they could not believe that she did not pass out. That was her first time using the power given to her by the Holy Spirit to heal her.

In March of 2008, she joined a travel company called World Ventures. Now, she was doing what she loves—selling art and working with the travel company. By this time, she had produced four cable TV shows and aired two, and she had several travel and art shows scheduled. On October 8, 2008, Keeley was going to pick her up to go to a travel meeting. The night before, at 1:00 a.m., she had the worst headache she had ever had in the back of her head. She got dressed, and Keeley picked her up at 10:30 a.m. She had asked Keeley to bring Tylenol because she still had the headache. When she came down to the car, Keeley told her that her hair was not combed and her top was inside out. She had looked in the mirror before coming down to the car, and she thought she looked fine. She went back to fix herself, and they went to the meeting. While there, she was not herself and it was noticeable to everyone and she still had the headache after taking three Tylenols. The meeting was over at 11:30 a.m., and all she wanted to do was go home and lie down. But Keeley did not like the way she looked and called her doctor and told him her symptoms, and he said, "Get her to the hospital, she is having a stroke." Keeley called her family and friends. Her mother, Mildred, would arrive in a few days. Keeley came by every day, and the next morning when she came, she did not like what she saw—Kim was feeding herself. Keeley is a calm, kind person, but she called the nurses in and laid them out and then called the director of nursing and told her that Kim better not look like that again.

CHAPTER 2

The Hospital

EVERY MORNING, SHE would read her Bible and a book called *Walking in God's Word (Through His Promises)*. She would read all the scriptures on healing and a book that a friend gave her that included scriptures. The inside cover reads,

> Dear Kim, the words of this book come straight from the heart of Jesus, they are treasures from heaven given to you to encourage you, help strengthen you and uplift you in your relationship with him. He died for you on the cross and with his word he crosses our hearts. May you be forever blessed and forever changed by the redeeming nature of his word and his love. God bless you.

Second Timothy 1:7 (NKJV) became her foundation: "God has not given us a spirit of fear but of power and of love and of a sound mind." This book blessed her then, and it continues to do so today.

After a few days in the hospital she began to have the feeling of water on her fore head and left arm. She would take a towel and wipe them off and the towel would be dry. This happened 2 to 3 times a day. She asked her mother to feel the towels and she said that they were dry and she asked the nurses and her friends to feel the towels and they said that they were dry. She asked her doctor about the water sensation and he did not know why it was happening. She even let the towels pile up in the chair for The cleaning people to feel and they said they were dry. She just wanted to know what the water sensation was about. Finally, she told her sister VernIce about it and she asked some of the doctors at the hospital where she works in philadelphia and they told her that the water sensation were her nerves coming back to life. Thank God she was happy to have an answer.

Her doctors and nurses were great. Her doctor would ask her daily who Vernice Wooden was. She called every day and asked a lot of questions. She was very knowledgeable. She said that Vernice was her sister and that she was in the medical field. "Every family should have a person like her. She is our medical advocate."

She went to physical, speech, and occupational therapy every day. She was fortunate to have had many visitors. Sometimes, the nurse would come by and tell them to quiet down. Some of her friends had some funny stories about things that she said when they came, which she didn't remember. This is Sharon's story:

I remember receiving a phone call I wasn't expecting. This was on a sunny day, and I had been with my oldest daughter, shopping. The caller was my daughter's father. I said hello, and I did not expect to hear what he had to say. It was as though time stood still. "Kim Blackwell is in the hospital. She had a stroke. I am not sure how bad it is, but I knew you would want to know."

I stopped everything. How could this be happening? Kim was not a heavy drinker. Sure, she was a social drinker as I am. Heck, she worked out. She was one of my closest friends who seemed to have her act together. You know the type, the sister that has every short cropped hair in place and outfits always together, so all I could think of as my daughter drove me the long drive was, *How could this happen?* So young, she had good eating habits, etc. Kim and I always had a special relationship, the type where you can keep each other's secrets, share each other's drama, and keep it real with one another. I value our relationship. We even went through our D word—divorce—along the same timeline, dissolving a four-party friendship to become two and two. I worried and prayed all the way from San Bernardino County (I resided in Chino Hills) to San Fernando Valley, not knowing what to expect. Boy, was I surprised.

As my daughter Lei Anna and I entered the hospital wing toward the direction the staff pointed where we would find my friend, I suddenly heard a familiar voice coming from the direction we were headed. A loud voice rang out. Yes, it was Kim, not at all what I expected. I thought that since I had been told she had suffered not one but two strokes on the table at her arrival, let's just put it out there, I just knew she would be near dead, you know, wires, IV, heart and respiration monitors. But oh no, not Kim. This strong-willed middle-aged black woman was barking orders and taking names as only she could. Kim said, "You people better get me out of this bed. I'm not using no darn bedpan. Are you crazy? Oh, but when Mildred gets here, my mama is going to make you guys listen to me." I couldn't believe my ears or my eyes.

I asked her if she was okay. She said, "Why? Don't I look okay?" I noticed her speech was a little slurred, and she had little to no movement on her left side. But I also noticed she was not about to let a stroke or a couple of strokes stop or hinder her in any way. Kim Blackwell was more determined to be the whole Kim Blackwell, stroke or not. Now, it was my turn. I said, "Kim, can I help you with anything?" Why did I ask that stupid question? She began to give me orders.

"Don't just stand there. You see my hair. I need for you to comb my hair. I need some barrettes, bobby pins, or something. Make it look nice. They got me looking crazy up in here."

My daughter and I looked at each other. Barrettes, bobby pins—it had to be the stroke. Kim always wore her hair in some latest cut. The Kim I knew and loved would never be caught dead with barrettes in her do. But she continued that I had to hook her hair up, stating, "You know I got to have my hair combed. Why has no one combed my hair up in here?" I laughed and combed her hair, making her look as presentable as possible; after all, she acted as though Obama himself was going to be dropping in to pay her a visit. "I just suffered a stroke, but I got to look good." Who else but Kim!

As if the hair fiasco wasn't enough, Kim decided that as her entrusted and longtime friend, she would trust me, Sharon, to have the pleasure and great honor of seeing that she be placed on the potty that she rang the bell and requested the nurses to bring in. Kimberly Blackwell was animate; she was not going to use a bedpan. So she turned to me and said, with a slightly twisted mouth, "We've been friends long enough. You can see my ass. So help me get out of this damn bed and put me on the pot. I think I have to go, and I can use it while you visit me." Well, I have my marching orders; with the help of my daughter, we were able to get her out of the bed and onto the pot. I enjoyed her attitude so much. She took away my fears I had about recovering. Kim has, to my knowledge, always been a fighter. There was no doubt in my mind she would do exactly as she said, while sitting on that pot. "They say I'm not going to walk again, I'm not going to be the same, I'm not going to recover from this. They don't know me. They don't know what I know. They don't know my God, and they sure don't know my mama. Wait till Mildred gets here."

I write this with all the love in my heart for my friend, my sister, Kim Blackwell, whom I speak with on a daily basis and who is an inspiration to us all, who expected whatever setbacks she has had and continues to fight her way through and continues to have a positive attitude and is here to tell her story of what believing in one's self and God can do.

I love you, Kim. Sharon.

Now, let her paint this picture for you: everything is different. She had to learn how to do everything again. We take everything for granted. (She doesn't anymore.)

She had to train her muscles to be able to function again, including her butt muscles once she was able to get to the toilet with her walker, with a wheelchair, or with a nurse helping her. Imagine going to the bathroom to move your bowels and you can't move them the way you used to. That was a surprise. You go in there and you think it's going to be a fifteen-minute process, and it takes thirty minutes. She had to learn how to eat without drooling and how to put her clothes on. She was discharged October 31, in time to walk to the polls to vote for President Barack Obama. That was a great day because she walked to the polls and voted for the first African American president. Her friends and family would tell her how much of a miracle she was, but when three neurologists told her, it confirmed what her family had said. One said that she should not be here after looking at the MRI of her brain. The next one said that she must know God and she said yes, she does, and the final one said it was a miracle that she recovered.

CHAPTER 3

Therapy

California and Philadelphia

California

SHE DID TWO months of speech, occupational, and physical therapy as an outpatient. Barbara was her speech therapist. Speech therapy is more than working on improving your speech; she did exercises to strengthen muscles and to practice talking slower and to project her words. It should be called cognitive therapy because you're teaching your brain how to process information and solve problems by working on your short-term and long-term memory, and doing word problems and math problems. She was given a lot of homework to do, and quite frankly, she felt like she was in the fifth grade. She did all her homework and everything asked of her because her goal was to get better. She came to therapy with that mind-set and attitude that she acquired in 1990, from recovering from her knee injury. Barbara would say, "Kim, you are one of my best patients."

Philadelphia

She was glad to be back in Philadelphia with her family, and she knew that being there played a big part in her speedy recovery. It was a family affair. She stayed with her mother for three months and her brother for four months. While in Philadelphia, she got to be a part of the things she missed being in California, such as family gatherings, birthday celebrations, and holidays. It was a joy to be there. Her niece and nephew helped her with her exercises daily and were very encouraging. Her nephew Trey came home from school with things that he made that would help improve the mobility of her left hand. While in Philadelphia, she had speech, occupational, and vision therapy for seven months. Speech therapy in Philadelphia was different. She read books, newspapers, and magazines because that worked on her short- and long-term memory and comprehension and also helped improve her vision. During this time, she read quite a few books by people who had strokes. Some survived and some did not. There was a common theme throughout all the books that she read, and that was the loss of their independence. What a major impact it had on their lives. After extensive therapy, some returned to their jobs and others did not.

Her vision therapy was with a neuro-optometrist. Her visual impairment was with her left visual field. In Philadelphia, her brother took her to empty parking lots to practice driving because she did not want to be afraid to get behind the wheel. At the end of seven months of therapy, her visual field had to be 90 percent, but she was only at 20 percent.

With occupational therapy, she learned to cook, wash and dry dishes, wash and fold clothes, and sweep and mop floors. Her last assignment before she was discharged was she had to make a full dinner. So she went shopping with her mother and pushed the shopping cart and picked up all the items that she needed to prepare the meal. She made a chicken salad and rice; then she washed, dried, and put away the dishes and mopped the floor. This may sound like minor things to do, but they were major accomplishments.

There was an intern named Larry; he was a great guy with a lot of patience. He worked with her on folding clothes. Some days she just did not feel like doing it. Folding sheets was difficult and still is today. Larry would say, "Kim, do you like the way that looks?" She would say to herself, *I don't care*, then she would do it again. She finished her therapy in Philadelphia in July 2009. Before she came back to California, she and her mother went on a cruise to Alaska. It is a beautiful place. That was in July, and the weather was gorgeous.

California

Her new life. Her mother came back with her and stayed two months to make sure that she would be okay. By this time, the state disability had expired, so she had health insurance and no income. She was in a state of despair; she did not know what to do. She got on the phone with the state disability office almost in tears talking to a lady about what to do. (She had worked all her life) the lady said, "Don't worry now, you file for Social Security disability." She went to the Social Security office and filed in September 2009. In the meantime, she had health insurance and no income. But thank God that she was smart enough to have invested in her own IRAs while selling insurance and investments to others. A friend told her to go down to the county for a doctor and medication. She went to the county, and this is where she saw how the system works. She was there for six hours, waiting to see someone so that she could get into the system to receive medication and to see a doctor. Now if you're pregnant, you can see somebody right away. If you have kids, you get the benefits immediately, but even if you're sick but not sick enough to go to the emergency room, you still have to wait. After all that, it took two months to get to see a doctor, but she got her medicine right away. What about income? She had to use her IRAs and 401(k) from the *Los Angeles Times*.

Then she got her first denial letter from Social Security. She filed an appeal and was denied. On October 8, 2009, one year later the exact date, Keeley came over to celebrate her one-year recovery anniversary. That day, she had a seizure and she called 911, and she was taken back to Providence Holy Cross Medical Center. Her doctor said that this type of seizure was rare because it was a direct result from having a stroke. Mildred came back out to take care of her. She was in the hospital for four days. She thanked God for her friends; Keeley took charge. Her mother was not going to get there for two days, so Keeley called her friends and put everybody on a schedule to help out. It filled her heart to see how wonderful they were. Keeley said, when she called each one, they said, "What do you want me to do?" Keeley said, "All we have to do is take care of things until Mildred gets here." Kim's COBRA health insurance would expire on October 12. She was discharged on October 14; she only had to pay for two days. God is good. She filed another appeal. Now, she has had a stroke and a seizure, and she had doctors' letters and medical records from therapists in Philadelphia and California; she got denied again. Now, she realized that this was a game that she did not know how to play. So she got a Social Security disability attorney—Binder & Binder. Kim recommends getting an attorney after her first denial. At the same time, she lost her independence. She could not drive, so she needed transportation. She found a local transportation that took her to all her doctors and to the various hospitals in the area, and that was good. She had wonderful friends. Keeley committed to take her to church once a month. Tammy, Karyn, and Brenda would take her shopping and on other outings.

Then she applied for Access, which is a 24 hour ride share program that operates 365 days. Once again, she gathered all her records, doctors' notes, and Social Security certificate stating that she was disabled and went down to take the evaluation for Access. She was denied and she appealed and she was denied because she could get on the bus and walk around the track. She could not believe it. She has had a stroke and a seizure, and she could have a seizure at any time and she was having mini-seizures often. She needed to have a guaranteed seat. And with the stroke, she had balance issues and got disoriented. Tammy told her about a lady at her church. "Maybe she can help you. I will get her phone number and tell her that you'll call her." *My God shall supply all my needs,* thought Kim. The next day, the lady called her and said, "Kim, I understand that you're having problems getting Access."

She said, "Yes, I am."

The lady said, "Don't worry. I am on the board of disabilities [look at God], so I will call them and they will call me back. There are a lot of people like you, Kim, that can't see their disability on the outside."

One hour later, a man called from Access and said, "Kim, I heard that you're having a problem getting Access. Don't worry, you are what they call a category one, so get another application and explain in detail why you cannot get on the bus or train and how your impairments prevent you from doing that. Then go down for another evaluation and call me when you're finished."

She did that, and after her evaluation, a girl said, "I guess you know you passed and you will get your card in two weeks."

She called the man back when she finished; he said, "Kim, you will have your card next week." She did not realize that the decisions were made on such a low level.

When she told the girl she was a category one and gave her four pages explaining her situation, the girl looked surprised. She asked her, "Don't you know what that is?"

The girl said, "Yes, but I did not think that you knew." Like they say, it is not what you know but who you know.

She hired Binder & Binder, the Social Security disability attorneys, to represent her. The file date would be the first day that she applied, which was September 2009. It was a long, hard road. She went through her 401(k) from the *Los Angeles Times* and two IR As. After two years, she got a hearing; her good friend Randy took her to the hearing. She was standing in front of the judge, who said, "You look really young. How have you been living?" She told her that she was living off her 401(k) and IR As. The judge looked surprised and asked the doctor from Social Security what he thought.

He said, "I have read her files and medical reports, and I do not think she will be able to work again between the seizures and her left arm and hand impairments and her vision."

Two years later, they won her case in 2011. They paid back pay from September 2009. She paid the attorneys, paid off two credit cards, paid her tithes, and put money in the bank. In April, Tammy got a job when Kim got Access. She is such a blessing; God had made her available to help her the whole time. She got Social Security disability, Access for transportation, a Yorkie named Maddie, and a wonderful man. His name is Michael Phelps; he is a very talented artist. She got her independence back, and she was so grateful.

Her days consist of prayer in the morning. She reads her devotional from a book titled *My Utmost for His Highest*; she reads the book her friend gave her in the hospital, *Walking in God's Word (Through His Promises)*, and the newspaper daily. She walks every day and cooks her meals and does exercises to improve her hand. She does have mini-seizures that are jerks in her left hand and shoulder, twitches of the left arm, and sometimes closure of the left hand. She believes in the power of the Holy Spirit. So when the seizures occur, she prays in the spirit. Jesus said that he would leave us a helper who would comfort us and guide us into all truths. She has stopped her seizures by praying-in the spirit. She is a hearer and a doer of the Word of God.

In Philadelphia, she went on a bus trip to see a play with her mother. During the intermission, they were out in the hall, and she had a seizure. She felt it coming. It started with a warm sensation coming up the left side of her back. Her left arm and hand started jerking and twitching. She remained calm because her mother had never seen it happen. Her mother asked what was wrong, and she walked off to the side and started to pray in tongues. Her mother was concerned, and the woman who gave the trip came over to her to ask if she was okay and if she needed to go to the hospital. Now, there was a bus full of people waiting. She asked God to help her and continued to pray in tongues until the seizure stopped. It took about fifteen minutes, and then they went back in to watch the play.

Maddie had seizures, and every morning, she would pray over her, and when she would have a seizure, she would pick her up and pray in tongues over her.

The Holy Spirit is her power source, and she uses it. She thanks God for Jesus and the Holy Spirit.

Now, she has recovered fully. There are still some issues, such as a weakness in her left hand, and she continues to have mini-seizures sometimes, but the blessing is that she has a sound mind and she is here writing this book. Who would have thought that from her fiftieth birthday until now, so much has happened?

She will celebrate her sixtieth birthday this year, 2017, in New Orleans with friends.

During this new life, there have been a lot of things that God has done by his grace for her, and he showed her that he is always there. There is a song by Vashawn Mitchell called "His Love." Some of the lyrics are, "There is nothing like his love / it's always there / it never gives up / it never runs out / there is nothing like his love."

CHAPTER 4

He's Always There

HERE ARE SOME examples of her *He's always there* experiences.

Let's start with Keeley deciding to drive to the travel meeting and making the decision to call Kim's doctor when she wanted to go home and lie down. Then God had her girlfriends available to help her at one point. Keeley, Karyn, and Tammy were laid off and were available to help her. Keeley was at her house when she had the seizure and when she was sent back to the hospital on October 8, 2009. Her COBRA health insurance expired October 12, 2009, and she was discharged from the hospital on October 14, 2009. She only had to pay for two days of that hospital bill.

She used to go to Philadelphia every year for Christmas to visit her family. She would always try to get a flight that did not stop in Chicago. Unfortunately, this time, she could not avoid it. She had a one-and-a-half-hour layover in Chicago. When she landed, they announced that the plane was going to be delayed coming out of Philadelphia, so it would take another hour. She decided to go to the restaurant and get something to eat. There were no seats available. There was a lady sitting at a table, and she offered her to sit down at her table. She was heading to Philadelphia also. She sat down, and her name was Grace. She was a very nice lady. They talked about their lives and other things. But then there was an announcement that the plane was going to be delayed again. She was very tired, so she went back to the gate to sit down. People were everywhere, sitting on the floor and in the aisles. So she went to the next gate and sat down. She fell asleep, and then she felt a hard push on her back. She turned around to see who had pushed her, and there was no one there. She rushed back to the gate, and everyone was gone. She went to the desk and asked the lady where everyone was. The lady said, "Ms. Blackwell, your plane is getting ready to leave." She rushed down to the plane, when she entered, she saw Grace. Grace said, "That's her. That's Kim Blackwell." She said, "Kim, I told them that I knew you and that you were coming, please don't leave her." As soon as she sat down and the plane pulled off, she knew that that push on her back was an angel sent by God.

Her dog, KJ, sometimes would go into the kitchen and pee on the floor before she put a gate in front of it. She was getting ready to go to bed and realized he had done that, so she went to the bathroom and prepared to clean it up. She pulled up the stopper in the sink and ran water. She cleaned up the mess and went to bed. It was about midnight. The next morning, she came down at 7:00 a.m. and opened the door to the bathroom, and it was steamy and the water was still running. That was seven hours later. But there was not one drop of water on the floor or counter; she could not believe it. She fell to her knees and wept. Sometimes, God is so good to her it is overwhelming. There was no way that the water should not have run over, only by the grace of God. He's always there. It was a Saturday afternoon. Maddie had a seizure, and she prayed over her and stopped it. Another one started again, and it lasted a while. She had just had one on Tuesday of that week. She had been thinking about what she should do because they were happening so often. She had just started a new seizure medication. Her type of seizures was called idiopathic seizures, meaning they happen for no reason. She could not continue to let Maddie suffer. She called Tammy, who said, "I will be there right away." God made her available to buy

Maddie with her, and she was with her to put her down. She was glad she was available because it was very hard. Maddie was like her child.

Finally, she was shopping at the mall, and she went to a store and bought something, which was placed in a small bag, then she went to JCPenney. In her arms, she had two pairs of pants and a top, a small bag in her hand, and her purse on her left shoulder as she was walking toward the dressing room. She dropped everything. She started to panic; she grabbed everything to put back in the small bag and picked up the pants and thought she had everything and went to the dressing room. She got inside and put everything down, and she did not have her purse. She rushed back outside to find it. Now, she was really panicking. There was a woman heading toward her, and she said, "Miss, I saw you drop everything. I have your purse. I was coming to find you. Don't worry." She gave her the purse, and Kim began to tell her that she had a stroke and that she got disoriented and had some vision issues. The woman said, "I understand. My mother had a stroke. Don't worry. It's okay, everything is fine." She went back to the dressing room and wept. The Bible says that he will never leave us nor forsake us and he is always there.

CHAPTER 5

The Access Experience

SHE IS SO grateful to have Access for her transportation. She has gotten back her independence. She can go anywhere in Los Angeles County. Since she got the service, she has met many church members that she would have never met. Since Access is a shared-ride service, she has met some very interesting people and have had some funny experiences.

You Are in My Seat

One day, she got picked up, and they had another stop. The lady got in, and she stood next to her, waiting and looking at her. Then she said, "You are in my seat."

Kim said, "Excuse me?"

The woman said, "You are in my seat," and continued to stand there like she was waiting for her to get up.

The driver said, "What is the matter, Miss?"

She said again, "She is in my seat."

He said, "Miss, please take a seat so that we can leave." She was upset, but she finally sat down.

The Cat Ladies

Kim loves dogs, but she does not like cats. She has a love-hate relationship with cats; they have always been a problem in her complex as long as she has lived there. It is a love-hate relationship because she knows the good they do. They keep mice, rats, and other rodents away, but she has a problem when they come on her patio. She has had her screen door damaged one time. Their smell was so strong that she did not want to sit out on her patio. She had a lot of strays, so she started to trap some and send them to the pound. She was trapping one to two cats a week. Now she was doing the right thing.

One day, she got a call from Animal Care and Control asking her what she was doing. They said something to the effect of, "Are you doing this as a hobby?" She couldn't believe her ears.

She said, "What I work?" She just did not want all these cats around. She said all that to say she knew the cat smell. So when the two ladies got in the van and she smelled a strong cat smell, she prayed that they would be dropped off first. One lady had a black coat on that was covered with cat hair. The other lady had on a black blouse covered in cat hair. The cat smell was so strong she was going to ask the driver to open a window, but he already had. Thank God that they were dropped off first, and immediately the smell was gone.

Thelma and the Oxygen Tanks

Thelma was one of her church members that she met on Access, whom she would have never met. She lived close to her, so sometimes they would ride home together. When they got in the van, there was a man in a wheelchair that had four oxygen tanks attached to it. They said hello and sat down. Then Thelma asked the man, "Do you always have this many oxygen tanks?" The man did not respond. She asked him again; he still did not respond. Now, we were at Thelma's house, and her brother came out of the house, smoking a cigarette, and he was headed toward the van. Thelma shouted, "Go back, go back! We have oxygen tanks in here." That had been her funniest experience to date.

Access will never leave you stranded.

Kim had to call twenty-four hours in advance to make a reservation. This time, she was going to a memorial service for her girlfriend Karyn's mother. She called and gave the dispatcher the address to the church and said it was in Los Angeles. She said she did not see the address listed in Los Angeles, so she insisted that it was in Compton. As they were driving, she looked at her surroundings. The exit they got off on looked like a bad area. When the driver got to the address, it was an auto repair yard, and it was very dark. She told the driver that she was not going to get out of the car because she did not feel safe. Their job was to drop passengers off at the address that they were given. But she refused to get out, and he understood why. He called the dispatch operator to tell them that she wanted to be taken home. He explained that the area was not where she was supposed to be and she agreed. He would not leave her here. It was not safe; she wanted to go back home. He talked to the supervisor and told him the same thing, and they gave him the approval to take her home. When she talked to Karyn that night, she said that she was only five minutes away. There were a lot of cities like that. For example, she lived in the city of San Fernando, and once you cross over a street called Hubbart, you are in Sylmar.

You call yourself a Christian?

This was at a time when she was not being so nice. Her pickup time was at 1:00 p.m. from the beauty school. She called for an ETA because their twenty minutes had passed. A van pulled up; the driver got out, and she had a clipboard in her hand. The woman walked over to her and asked her, "Are you Kim Blackwell?" She said yes, and the woman saw her name on the clipboard. She walked over to the van. The driver got out, but she did not open the door for her. She got back in the van and looked at the computer and started to pull the van out of the parking space. She asked her where she was going. She pointed to the computer. She did not speak good English and she said, "Your name not in here."

She said, "What do you mean? You saw my name on your clipboard?" The driver continued to back the van out of the space.

She said, "You better not leave me." That scared her. Then another van pulled up, and she thought it was for her. But, oh no, she went to console the driver. Her driver got in the van, and they were in there ten more minutes. In the meantime, no one was telling her anything. So she went over to the van, and the supervisor said, "We are going to send another van for you."

She asked the supervisor what happened because she saw her name on her clipboard. The supervisor said, "Yes, she had you as a pickup, but dispatch pulled it from her and did not give it to another driver. Another van will be here for you in twenty minutes."

Now it was 3:00p.m. She went over to the other driver to say that she was sorry when she found out what happened. But she would not look or talk to her. She was not acting like Jesus that day.

CONCLUSION

REMEMBER THAT A successful recovery starts with you. First, you must have the desire, courage, and will to get better. Second, your attitude must always be of gratefulness. Third, you must be motivated to do what you are told to do. Fourth, you must accept your new life, always remembering how blessed you are to be alive. Finally, recovery cannot be done alone; you must believe in God and stay in his Word daily.

Here Is the Process

Once you are admitted into the hospital, you are assigned a caseworker. Make sure that person is working for you and with you, keeping you informed. Before you are discharged, have the caseworker get you the forms to file for state disability income. This will give you an income for one year if you have consistently worked. When you file, they will let you know if you are eligible. After one year, you can file for Social Security disability income. Keep good records such as letters from your doctors and anything pertaining to your health. Obtain your medical records so that you can read them and find out everything that happened to you in the hospital, and you will have them for future reference. Once you file for Social Security disability income, depending on the severity of your disability, you may be denied. There is no up-front fee. Most attorneys, if they win the case, that is when they get paid. And if they do not win, they will make arrangements for you to pay them.

Transportation

Most cities provide transportation for the disabled, such as Dial-a-Ride, and there is Access Paratransit and other services like it. Apply for Access right away. While you are waiting to get Social Security disability, you will need to see doctors and get your medicine, so go to the county in your city. Every day, stay in the Word of God to keep yourself uplifted.

Contact the various associations such as the American Heart Association, the National Stroke Association, and others. Utilize the support groups that are available. Kim attended a few stroke-recovery classes and found it to be informative and comforting to be with other stroke survivors. She learned a lot and realized how blessed she was to be there. There will be times when you are frustrated by what you cannot do, and you think about all the things that you used to be able to do. Just remember how blessed you are that you survived and that God is always there.

Her prayer is for everyone who reads this book to find it helpful in the recovery of their lives or of someone they know. God wants us to tell our story.

This is Kim Monica Blackwell, *a child of the living God*. (All scriptures are taken from the New King James version of the Bible)

APPENDIX 1

Scriptures She Confessed Daily

Psalm 107:20 (NKJV)
He sent his word and healed them

2 Timothy 1:7 (NKJV)
God has not given us a spirit of fear but of power and of love and of a sound mind. (This became her foundation Scripture.)

Philippians 4:6 (NKJV)
Be anxious for nothing but in everything by prayer and supplication with thanksgiving, let your requests be made known to God.

Proverbs 3:5–6 (NKJV)
Trust in the Lord with all your heart, and lean not on your own understanding, in all your ways acknowledge him, he shall direct your paths.

Deuteronomy 31:8 (NKJV)
And the Lord, he is the one who goes before you, he will be with you, he will not leave you, nor forsake you, do not fear nor be dismayed.

Ezra 7:28 (NKJV)
I was encouraged as the hand of the Lord my God was upon me.

Isaiah 55:11 (NKJV)
So shall my word be that goes from out of my mouth, it shall not return to me void, but it shall accomplish what I please and it shall prosper in the thing for which I sent it.

Jeremiah 29:11 (NKJV)
For I know the thoughts that I think towards you, says the Lord, thoughts of peace and not of evil to give you a future and a hope.

Jeremiah 1:5 (NKJV)
Before I formed you in the womb I knew you, before you were born I sanctified you, I ordained you a prophet to the nations.

Psalms 103:2–3 (NKJV)
Bless the Lord, O my soul, and forget not all his benefits:
who forgives all your iniquities, and heals all your diseases.

APPENDIX 2

Songs that Comforted Her

Marvin Sapp
> "I Believe"

Smokie Norful
> "I Understand"

Fred Hammond
> "I Press"

Donnie McClurkin
> "Stand"
>
> "Who Would've Thought"

Vashawn Mitchell
> "Give All I Have"
>
> "Oh the Love"
>
> "Holy Spirit"
>
> "Secret Place"
>
> "God Will Take Care of Me"

APPENDIX 3

Books that Inspired Her

Books: *Walking in God's Word (Through His Promises)* by Frederick K. C. Price, DD

Daily Devotional: *My Utmost for His Highest* by Oswald Chambers

The New King James Version of the Bible

APPENDIX 4

Resources/Information

Disability Benefits

Medication Assistance

Transportation

What Causes a Stroke?

A stroke is a cardiovascular disease that affects the blood vessels supplying blood to the brain. A stroke occurs when a blood vessel bringing oxygen and nutrients to the brain bursts or is clogged by a blood clot or some other particle. Because of this rupture or blockage, part of the brain does not get the blood flow it needs. Deprived of oxygen, the nerve cells in the affected area of the brain cannot function and die within minutes. When nerve cells cannot function, part of the body controlled by these cells cannot function either. The devastating effects of a stroke are often permanent because brain cells are not replaced.

The above information is taken from the American Stroke Association Stroke Survivor and Caregiver Resource Guide 2005.

Stroke Risk Factors

There are various risk factors associated with stroke. There are three categories of risk factors:

Factors that cannot be controlled:

> Age: The risk for stroke increases with age.
>
> Sex: The incident of stroke is about 30 percent higher for men.
>
> Race: Black Americans have a 60 percent higher incidence of stroke than whites.
>
> Diabetes: A person with diabetes is more likely to have a stroke. If you have diabetes, it is important to follow a prescribed treatment program.
>
> A prior stroke: The risk of stroke is many times higher for someone who has had one.
>
> Heredity: People who have a family history of stroke are at a greater risk.

Factors that can be changed with medical treatment:

> High blood pressure: The risk varies directly with blood pressure. Controlling high blood pressure lowers risk of stroke significantly.
>
> Heart disease: People with heart disease have more than twice the risk of stroke than people with no heart problems.

Factors that can be changed with lifestyle:

> High cholesterol and triglyceride levels: It is important to follow a low-fat, low-cholesterol diet.

Cigarette smoking: Smoking cigarettes increases your risk of stroke.

Excessive alcohol intake: This can increase your blood pressure and weaken your heart.

Obesity: Excess weight increases your chances of having other risk factors for stroke such as high blood pressure, diabetes, and heart disease.

The above information is taken from the Stroke Association of Southern California.

Symptoms

Sudden numbness; weakness or paralysis of the face, arm, or leg on one side of the body; loss of speech; trouble talking or understanding speech; sudden dimness or loss of vision, particularly in one eye; unexplained dizziness; unsteadiness or sudden falls, especially in addition with any of the previous symptoms; sudden severe headache with no apparent cause, often described as the worst headache one has ever had.

Not all warning signs occur in every stroke patient. Don't ignore signs of stroke, even if they go away.

This information is taken from the Stroke Association of Southern California. Here are a few websites:

American Heart Association: www.aha.org or 800-242-8721 www.strokeassociation.org/strokeorg/warning signs Stroke.org www.heartorg/conditions

Disability Benefits

State Disability Insurance: If you temporarily cannot work because of an illness or injury that is not work or pregnancy related, you may be able to get state disability insurance (SDI). You must complete and mail a claim statement as an employee within forty-nine days of the date you became disabled. Contact 800-480-3287 for required forms and instruction.

Supplemental security income (SSI) is a cash benefit program for low-income persons sixty-five and over and for blind and disabled persons of any age. SSI has no work history requirement and provides medical eligibility.

To initiate the process, contact the Social Security office near you.

Social Security Disability (SSDI) is a federal insurance program that provides benefits for eligible workers and their families regardless of income. Monthly payments are made to you and eligible family members who have a record of covered employment who are unable to work because of severe, medically certified illness or other disability that has lasted or is expected to last at least twelve months or to end in death. SSDI provides Medicare eligibility and requires that the applicant have a record of covered employment in the ten years before becoming disabled. Contact 800-772-1213 or go to your nearest Social Security office.

The above information is taken from frequently requested resources by the clinical social work department of Providence health systems, San Fernando Valley service area, April 2009.

Social Security Disability planning: Go to https://ca.db101 programs.html

There are many Social Security disability attorneys. Check in your city for the best ones.

Kim used Binder & Binder: 800-662-4633. They were very good.

For general information for assistance in Los Angeles County, you can call the following phone numbers:

Burbank/Glendale: 818-956-1100

San Fernando Valley: 818-501-4447

Los Angeles: 213-686-0950

West Los Angeles: 213-551-2929

The above information is obtained from the clinical social work department of Providence health systems, San Fernando Valley service area, April 2009.

Medication Assistance

Medicare-Approved Discount Cards

Discount card price information and application can be obtained by calling 1-800-Medicare or by going to their website, www.medicare.gov/what medicare-covers/index. html

Retail pharmacy stores have pharmacy discount programs also:

Rite Aid savings card

CVS Health savings pass

Walgreens Prescription Savings Club

Rx Outreach: www.medicare.gov/what_medicare-covers/ index.html 800-769-3880. This program offers prescription medicines to uninsured individuals and those who have limited prescription drug coverage. Partnership for Prescription Assistance (888-477-2669, https://www.pparx.org/gethelp) helps qualifying patients without prescription drug coverage get the medicine they need through a program that is right for them.

Information provided by the clinical social work department of Providence health systems, San Fernando Valley service area (Frequently Requested Resources April 2009).

Transportation

Cityride (seniors and disabled adults)

Los Angeles:
    323-808-7433
    310-808-7433

San Fernando Valley:
    818-908-1901

Taxi services

San Fernando Valley:
    818-780-1000
    800-290-5600

Access Paratransit: 1-800-827-0829

(Information provided by frequently requested resources by the clinical social work department of Providence health systems, San Fernando Valley service area, April 2009.)

APPENDIX 5

Photos

Kim and Karyn in Brazil

Kim's fiftieth birthday in Barbados

Kim and Mildred in Venice, Italy

Wedding day, 1980

Chuks Okoye, Kim Blackwell, and George Nock

Front, Kim; *back row*, Tammy, Leslie, Joslyn, Mildred, Vernice, and Anna

Kim and Keeley

Pastor Cheryl Davis

Kim getting an award with PRIMERICA
Nelson Backwell, Sara Gutierrez, Kim, and Todd Walker

Kim's last day at the *Los Angeles Times*

Graduation 1979 from Duquesne University

Kim and Michael Phelps

Kim and her siblings

ENDURANCE

THIS PAINTING IS a tribute to the Black Woman for her devine legacy in contributing to the survival, growth and prosperity of all people of African decent, even in the most adverse conditions.

In this picture, I depict a classic circumstance where this extraordinary woman combines the cumulative impact of societal norms, spiritual devotion and cultural heritage to live up to the expectations of the family unit and her community, at large.

She majestically carries on the burden of life on her head with grace and poise, as she meditates over the teachings of her mother when she was young. The face of her mother is embedded on the lower part of her legs. She remembers what her mother taught her about what it takes to be an African mother- "The Ebony Tree". A tree that is known throughout the world for its strength, beauty, elegance and durability, no matter the environment it finds itself. This is the sign of the Black woman.

She is elegant, yet diligent to the pursuit of her cause;
...Enterprising, yet devoted to her mission in life;
...Gentle, yet strong in body and soul.

These characteristics can only be elevated by the support of a devoted soul mate. Hence, the figure of a man beside her. I also turned her legs into a tree trunk that spreads its roots to various directions, The maps of North America and Africa can be seen on both sides of the foregrounds. These two features symbolize the ties she has with her ancestral home in

Africa, while spreading her seeds of life and cultural heritage in various parts of the world, mostly in the "New World" of America.

There are four persons on the right hand side of the painting, which represents the extended family members, as well as her community at large. They see her unique qualities and the exemplary life she leads and honor her with their blessings and well wishes, which manifests as a dove. This is the bird shown over her head, dripping out the heavenly blessings on her body and her entire family.

We all must strive to emulate the characteristics of this woman, for keeping her dignity and grace under "fire", so that our families can continue to create that special bond amongst each other, which is inherent of the ancient traditional African family.

Chuks Echiemeze Okoye (BFA) A.D.200

Cover art By Chuks Okoye titled Endurance

Chuks Echiemize Okoye (BFA) A.D. 200

CHUKS ECHIEMEZE OKOYE BIOGRAPHY

CHUKS E. OKOYE was born in Jos, in Northern Nigeria. He began his Post Secondary education at University of Nigeria, Nsukka, in 1980. After a brief stay at the School of Fine and Applied Arts, where he was majoring in sculpture and African iconography, Chuks migrated to the United States of America. Continuing his studies in the United States, in 1983, Mr. Okoye obtained his Bachelor of Fine Arts degree from the University of Oklahoma in Norman, Oklahoma in 1987, with a major in product design and a minor in painting.

Chuks has chosen African and American art as his primary form of artistic expression by creating works of art in mixed-media, pencil, oil, and acrylic paintings. His recent venture into woodcarving and wall sculpture has earned him an extraordinary place in the art world as well. He has transformed this art form into framed wood collages and three-dimensional wall hangings, thereby creating a contemporary feel to this cultural reflection. The paintings and sculptures created by Chuks E. Okoye are distinctive, with a combination of realism and abstraction, using African beads and woven silk/rayon thread to make symbols and designs.

On canvas, this technique creates a three-dimensional effect. His art is a true representation of positive images that give rise to motivation and hope in ALL people. In fact, Chuks considers himself a pioneer in a new style of painting he calls "Abstract-Realism."

Chuks introduced these ideals to the world through his participation in numerous major art expos inclusive of the Kinfolk's expedition, Ramses and The African Origin of Civilization in Dallas, Texas; Black History Month celebration at the Epcot Center, Walt Disney World in Orlando, Florida; New York Art Expo, and the internationally recognized National Black Arts Festival in Atlanta, Georgia. As a Cultural Ambassador of his native country in Nigeria, his artworks were selected to be used in decorating the walls of the Embassy of Nigeria in Washington D.C. and the Consulate offices in Atlanta, Georgia.

In 1990, Chuks' artwork was featured in both the Dallas Observer and the Dallas Morning News. Among some of the numerous articles of features about Mr. Okoye and his works of art were the publications in the Art Business news, September, 1998; Good News magazine, April, 2001 and Upscale magazine in May 2001. He was also selected by Bentley House Publishing Group to be one of the featured artists in its "African-American Collection" and shares this honor with other artistic notables such as Charles Bibbs, Leroy Campbell, Paul Goodnight, Brenda Joysmith, and Poncho Brown, to name a few.

Mr. Chuks Okoye has appeared on various television and radio interview/shows, in Dallas and Houston, Texas; Los Angeles, California; Chicago, Illinois; Atlanta, Georgia; and Orlando, Florida.

His most recent exhibition is the "Echoes of the Past" at Terra Kulture at Victoria Island, Lagos, Nigeria. The grand opening was nationally televised on NTA Nigeria. One of his most recent accolades includes winning the "Best of Show" Award at New Orleans Jazz and Heritage Festival, Congo square marketplace May 2014. And Award of Excellence at the Kissimmee, Florida annual Art festival, August 2014.

Studio- 770 478-7044
Address 8521 Plumtree, Dr. Riverdale GA 30274
E mail address: chuks@apelart.com

In Memory Of Robin Mcconnell

www.ingramcontent.com/pod-product-compliance
Lightning Source LLC
Chambersburg PA
CBHW030131100526
44591CB00009B/598